Piano/Vocal

Broadway Best

SONGBOOK

ISBN 0-7935-2118-1

HAL•LEONARD®
CORPORATION
7777 W. BLUEMOUND RD. P.O. BOX 13819 MILWAUKEE, WI 53213

Broadway Belter's
SONGBOOK

Contents

And All That Jazz

from CHICAGO

Words by FRED EBB
Music by JOHN KANDER

Broadway Baby

from FOLLIES

Words and Music by
STEPHEN SONDHEIM

Cabaret
from CABARET

Music by JOHN KANDER
Words by FRED EBB

Allegro - In 2

Piano

poco rit. *molto rit.* (arp. E7) (ad lib.)

Moderate 2

SALLY:

What good is sit-ting a-lone in your room?_ Come hear the

mu-sic play. Life is a cab-a-

cab - a - ret, old chum,___ Come to the cab - a -

Slightly faster

ret!_____ I used to have a

girl-friend known as El - sie, With whom I shared four

sor - did rooms in Chel - sea. She was-n't what you'd

call a blush-ing flow-er. As a mat-ter of fact she

rent-ed by the ho-ur. The day she died the

neigh-bors came to snick-er: "Well, that's what comes of

too much pills and li-quor." But when I saw her

Time for a hol - i - day.

Life is a cab - a - ret, old chum,

Come to the cab - a - ret." And as for

me, as for me, I made my

Come Rain or Come Shine

from ST. LOUIS WOMAN

Words by JOHNNY MERCER
Music by HAROLD ARLEN

Don't Rain On My Parade

from FUNNY GIRL

Words by BOB MERRILL
Music by JULE STYNE

— spill, It's me and not you. Who told you you're al - lowed to rain on my pa-

rade?

I'll march my band out, —

I'll beat my drum.

And if I'm

fanned out, —

Your turn at bat, sir, —

At

least I did-n't fake it. Hat, sir!— I guess I did-n't make it.

But wheth-er I'm the ___ rose Of sheer per-fec-tion, Or freck-le on the ___

___ nose Of life's com-plex-ion, The cin-der or the ___ shin-ey ap-ple of its

eye, _____ I got-ta fly once, I

28

love, 'Cause I'm a "com-er". I sim-ply got-ta___ march, My heart's a drum-mer.

Allargando-In 4

No-bod-y, no,__ no-bod-y Is gon-na rain on my pa-

Tempo I°

rade!

Down in the Depths
(on the Ninetieth Floor)

from RED, HOT AND BLUE!

Words and Music by
COLE PORTER

33

Everything's Coming Up Roses

from GYPSY

Words by STEPHEN SONDHEIM
Music by JULE STYNE

Get Out of Town
from LEAVE IT TO ME

Words and Music by
COLE PORTER

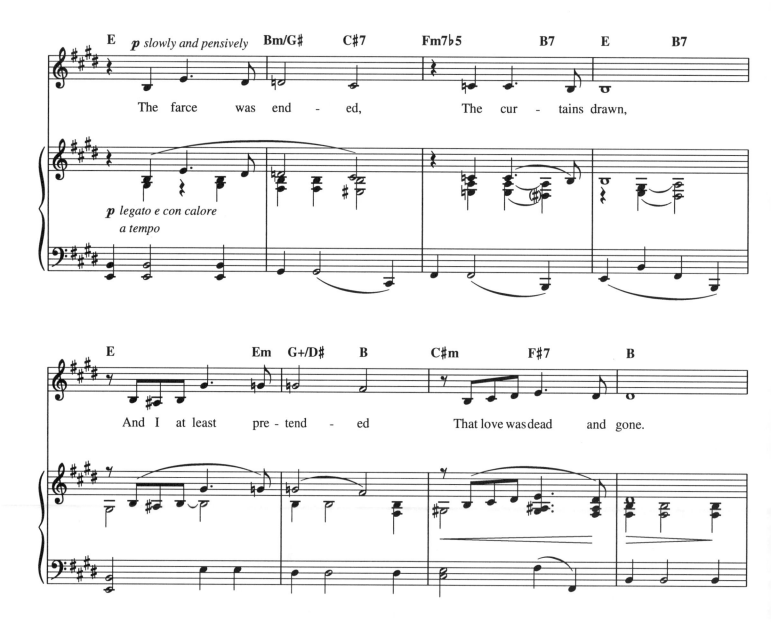

The farce was end - ed, The cur - tains drawn,

And I at least pre - tend - ed That love was dead and gone.

The Hostess With the Mostes'
on the Ball

from CALL ME MADAM

Words and Music by
IRVING BERLIN

Sally (ad lib.)

I was born on a thou-sand a-cres of Ok-la-ho-ma land

No-thing grew on the thou-sand a-cres for it was grav-el and sand

One day fath-er start-ed dig-ging in a field Hop-ing to find some soil He

dug and he dug and what do you think? Oil, oil, oil. The

slight rit.

colla voce

come and let his hair—down, Have the best time of his life— E - ven bring his new af-fair

—down, In - tro-duce her as his wife— But she must-n't leave her panties in the

hall. ——————— For the hos-tess who's the hos-tess, with the mos - tes'

on the ball. —————————————————————————

After Applause Segue Encore

Honey Bun
from SOUTH PACIFIC

Lyrics by OSCAR HAMMERSTEIN II
Music by RICHARD RODGERS

doll is as dain-ty as a spar-row___ Her fig - ure is some-thing to ap-

plaud. Where she's nar-row she's nar-row as an ar - row___ And she's

broad, where a broad, should be broad. _____ A

Allegretto

hun-dred and one Pounds of fun__ That's my lit-tle Hon-ey-Bun!

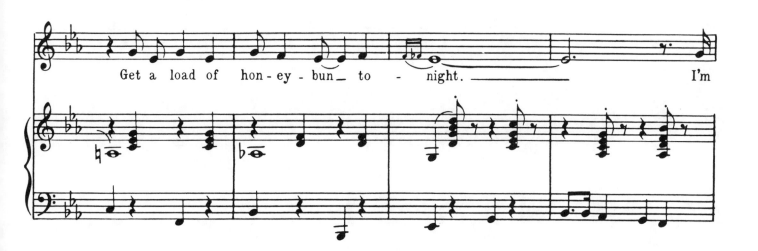

Get a load of hon-ey-bun__ to - night. _____ I'm

She's my ba - by, I'm her pap!_ I'm her boob-y, she's my trap!_

I am caught and don't want-a run,_ 'Cause I'm hav-in' so much

fun with Hon - ey - Bun! _____ A

f marcato

hun - dred and one pounds of fun_ That's my lit - tle Hon - ey - Bun!

pp

Get a load of hon-ey-bun to - night. _____ I'm

speak-in' of my Sweet-ie-Pie _ On - ly six - ty inch-es high

Ev-'ry inch is packed with dy - na - mite! _____ Her

hair is blonde and curl - y, Her curls are hurl - y burl - y. Her

lips are pips! I call her hips: "Twirl-y" and "Whirl-y"

(Danced)

(She's my ba - by, I'm her pap. I'm her boob - y

She's my trap.) I am caught and don't want-a run 'Cause I'm

hav - in' so much fun with Hon - ey - Bun.

f marcato

62

I'm Going Back

from BELLS ARE RINGING

Words by BETTY COMDEN
and ADOLPH GREEN
Music by JULE STYNE

They've got a great big switch-board there—

Where it's just "Hel - lo, good - bye."____ It

may be dull,__ But there I can be— just me, my - self and I.

A lit - tle mod'ling on the side. _____ Yes, that's where I'll

be _____ At the Bon - jour Tris - tesse

Bras - siere Com-pa - ny. _____ And if

an - y-bod - y asks for El - la, Me - la or Mom,

Tell them that I'm go-ing back where I came from, _ To the B. T. Bras-si - ère _

Com-pa - ny. _

Free   Broad and steady *(Sarah Vaughn style)*

Good-bye, ev'-ry-bod-y; Good-bye, Ma-dame Grim-al - di; Hp. Good-bye, Jun - ior Mal - let,

me, _____ To the Bon - jour Tris - tesse Bras - siere Com-pa - ny. ___

And

while I'm sit - tin' there I hope that I'll find out ___

Just what El - la Pe-ter-son is all a - bout, __ In that Shang - ri - la of

I Got the Sun in the Morning

from ANNIE GET YOUR GUN

Words and Music by
IRVING BERLIN

I Had Myself a True Love

from ST. LOUIS WOMAN

Words by JOHNNY MERCER
Music by HAROLD ARLEN

I'd Give My Life for You

from MISS SAIGON

Music by CLAUDE-MICHEL SCHÖNBERG
Lyrics by RICHARD MALTBY JR. and ALAIN BOUBLIL
Adapted from original French Lyrics by ALAIN BOUBLIL

I'll Be Seeing You

from RIGHT THIS WAY

Words by IRVING KAHAL
Music by SAMMY FAIN

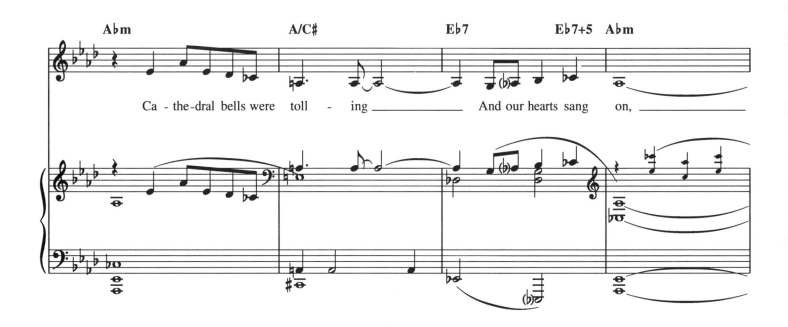

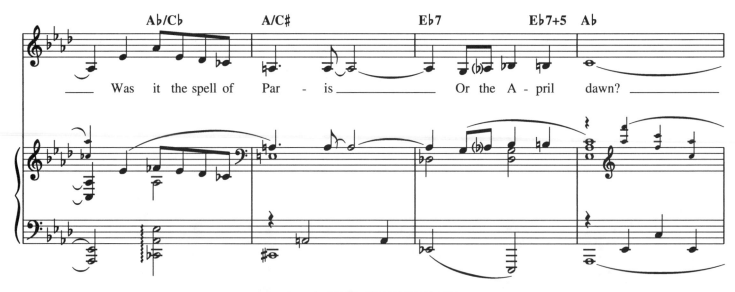

I'm the Greatest Star

from FUNNY GIRL

Words by BOB MERRILL
Music by JULE STYNE

think it's a plot 'cause they're scared that I've got such a gift. I'm miffed. 'Cause

Moderately - In 2

I'm the great-est star. I am by

far, But no one knows it. *(Spoken:)* Wait, they're gon-na hear a

(Sung:) voice _____ A sil-ver flute __ ah hah ah hah, They'll cheer each "toot" *(She applauds)*

When I ex - pose it! Can't you see to look at me That I'm a natch - ral "Ca - mille." As Ca - mille I just feel I've so — much to of - fer. I know I'd be di - vine be - cause I'm a nat - u - ral cough - er, (cough_____)

make 'em cry. I can make 'em sigh. Some-day they'll

Moderately slow - In 4

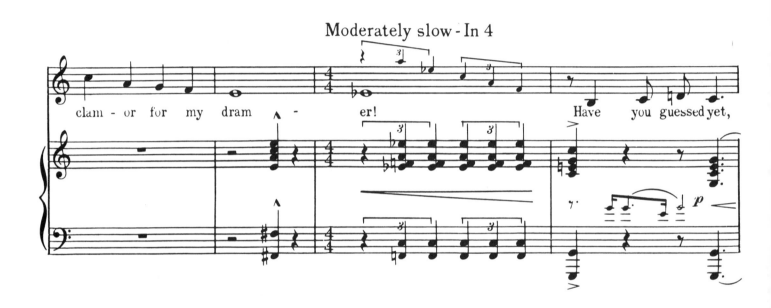

clam - or for my dram A - er! Have you guessed yet,

Not fast - In 2

Who's the best yet? If you ain't I'll tell you one more time.

You bet___ yer last dime, In all___ of the world so___ far___

___ i'm the great-est, great-est star!___

Dixieland

gliss *ff* Tutti *(notation ad lib.)*

ffz

I've Got You to Lean On

from ANYONE CAN WHISTLE

Words and Music by
STEPHEN SONDHEIM

Johnny One Note

from BABES IN ARMS

Words by LORENZ HART
Music by RICHARD RODGERS

stopped clap - ping, Traf - fic ceased its roar And_ they

tell us_ Ni - a - gra_ stood still!_____ He stopped the

train whis - tles, boat whis - tles, steam whis - tles, cop whis - tles,

All whis - tles bowed to_ his skill._____

110

So sing, John - ny one note,— out

loud! Sing, John - ny one note!—

Sing, John - ny one note,— out

loud!

The Lady Is a Tramp

from BABES IN ARMS

Words by LORENZ HART
Music by RICHARD RODGERS

Ca-'ad. But so-cial cir-cles spin too fast for me. _____ My

ho - bo - hem -ia is the place to be. _____

[In tempo]

I get too hun-gry for din - ner at eight. __
I go to Con - ey, The beach is di - vine. __

I like the thea-tre, but nev - er come late. __
I go to ball games, the bleach-ers are fine. __

I nev-er both-er with peo-ple I hate, —
I fol-low Win-chell and read ev-'ry line, —

That's why the la-dy is a tramp!
That's why the la-dy is a tramp!

I don't like crap games with bar-ons and earls. —
I like a prize fight that is-n't a fake. —

Won't go to Har-lem in er-mine and pearls. —
I love the row-ing on Cen-tral Park lake. —

116

Hate Cal - i - forn - ia, it's cold and it's damp, ___
I'm all a - lone when I low - er my lamp, ___

1.
That's why the la - dy is a tramp! _____

2.
That's why the la - dy is a

tramp. _____

Losing My Mind

from FOLLIES

Words and Music by
STEPHEN SONDHEIM

Does no one know? It's like I'm los-ing my mind.

All af - ter - noon, do - ing ev-'ry lit -tle chore, The thought of you stays

bright. Some-times I stand in the mid-dle of the floor,

Not go - ing left, Not go - ing right. I dim the lights

And think a-bout you, Spend sleep-less nights To think a-bout you You said you loved

me Or were you just be-ing kind? Or am I los-ing my

mind?

Memory

from CATS

Music by ANDREW LLOYD WEBBER
Text by TREVOR NUNN after T.S. ELIOT

a tempo

Day - light.___ I must wait for the sun - rise,___ I must think of a new life___ And I must-n't give

in._____ When the dawn comes to-night will be a me-mo-ry too___ And a

new day___ will be - gin.

125

Burnt out ends of smo-ky days,_____ the
stale cold smell ___ of mor-ning._____ The street lamp dies, an-o-ther

poco rit.

night is ov-er,___ an-o-ther day is dawn-ing.

poco rit.

126

My Funny Valentine
from BABES IN ARMS

Words by LORENZ HART
Music by RICHARD RODGERS

Moderately *(in 4)*

SUSIE:

Be - hold the way our fine feath - ered friend his vir - tue doth pa -

rade. Thou know - est not, my dim - wit - ted friend, the

pic - ture thou hast made. Thy va - cant brow and thy

tous - led hair con - ceal thy good in - tent. Thou

no - ble, up - right, truth - ful, sin - cere and slight - ly dope - y gent. You're

The Party's Over

from BELLS ARE RINGING

Words by BETTY COMDEN and ADOLPH GREEN
Music by JULE STYNE

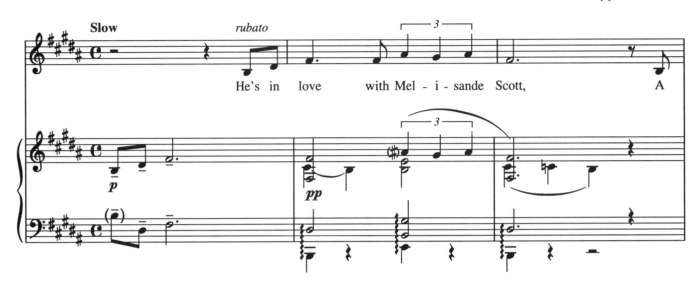

He's in love with Mel - i - sande Scott, A

girl who does - n't ex - ist. He's in love with some-one you're not, and

so, re-mem-ber, it was nev-er you he kissed. The par-ty's

You danced and dreamed through the night; It seemed to be right, just be - ing with him.

Now you must wake up; All dreams must end.

Take off your make-up. The par-ty's o - ver; It's all

o - ver, my friend.

Ridin' High

from RED, HOT AND BLUE!

Words and Music by
COLE PORTER

Love had socked me, sim-ply knocked me for ____ a loop.

Luck has dished me Till you fished me from ____ the soup.

Rose's Turn

from GYPSY

Words by STEPHEN SONDHEIM
Music by JULE STYNE

lights!

Play it, boys!

You ei - ther

got it   Or you ain't.   And boys, I   got   it! _

mp

ORCH:

ROSE:

You like it? (Yeah!)

Well, I got it.

Some peo-ple got it and make it pay.— Some— peo-ple can't e-ven give it a-way!—

This peo-ple's got it And this peo-ple's spread-in' it a-round.—

You ei - ther have it,

Or you've

had it.

Con moto (♩ = 120)

Hello, everybody! My name is Rose. What's yours?

mp

How d'ya like them egg rolls, Mister Goldstone?

Hold your hats and hal - le - lu - jah, Mom - ma's gon - na show it to ya.

Thanks a lot and out with the gar-bage. They take bows and you're bat-tin' ze-ro!

I had a dream.

I

dreamed it for you, June.

It

_ for my-self? Start-in' now it's gon - na be my turn! Gang-way, world, get off_

_ a' my run-way! Start-in' now, I bat a thou-sand! This time, boys, I'm tak-

Molto moderato (♩ = 92)

- in' the bows. And ev-'ry-thing's com- ing up Rose!

Ev-'ry-thing's com-ing up ros- es! Ev-'ry-thing's com-ing up

Some People

from GYPSY

Words by STEPHEN SONDHEIM
Music by JULE STYNE

Come on, Pop-pa, whad - da-ya say? Some peo - ple can

be con - tent__ Play - ing Bing - o and

pay - ing rent.__ That's peach - y for

some peo - ple, For some hum -

won-der-ful dream, Pop - pa!

All a-bout June and the Or-phe-um cir-cuit_ Give me a chance and I

know I can work it! I had a dream,_____

Just as re-al as can be, Pop - pa!

There I was in Mis-ter Or-phe-um's of-fice,—

And he was say-ing to me: "Rose!—

Get your-self some new__ or-ches-tra-tions, New rou-tines and red__

__ vel-vet cur-tains. Get a feath-ered hat__ for the ba-by,

all that I need is eight-y-eight bucks,

Pop-pa. That's what he said,

FATHER: You ain't gettin' eight cents from me, Rose. *(He exits)*

Pop-pa, On-ly eight-y-eight bucks,....

Repeat ad lib.

pp

Cue: ROSE: ...but I'll get it and get my kids out!

Tempo I° ($\quad$ = 120)

ROSE:

Good -

Tutti

mf

bye _____ To blue - ber - ry

pie! _____ Good rid - dance to

all the so - cials I___ had to go to, All the lodg - es I___

___ had to play, All the Shrin - ers I___ said hel - lo to___

Well, they can stay and rot,

But not Rose!

What Did I Have That I Don't Have?

from ON A CLEAR DAY YOU CAN SEE FOREVER

Words by ALAN JAY LERNER
Music by BURTON LANE

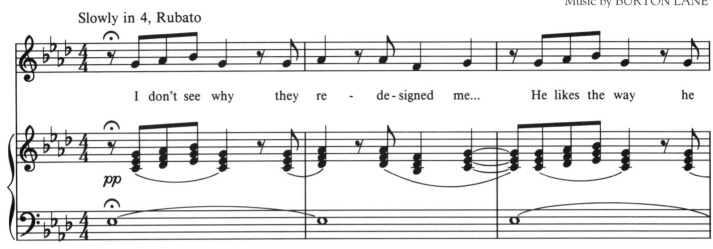

I don't see why they re - de-signed me... He likes the way he

used to find me. He likes the girl I left be - hind me.

I mean, he... I mean, me...

By my past.— What did he love that there's none of?—

What did I lose the sweet warm knack of? Would-n't I be the

late, great me If I knew how?_____ Oh!

What did I have I don't have now?

I'm not like? What was the charm that I've run dry of?

What would I give if my old know - how still knew

how! Oh! What did I have I

don't have now?

What Good Is Love

from PINS AND NEEDLES

Words and Music by
HAROLD ROME

Ev-'ry where I go I hear sweet songs a-bout the moon, Songs a-bout the stars a-bove and songs of love in June, Songs of hearts that beat as one to some sweet lov-er's tunes, But they're not songs that sing for me! Songs a-bout the dreams that lie with-

When You're Good to Mama

from CHICAGO

Words by FRED EBB
Music by JOHN KANDER

Don't you know that this hand __ wash - es that one
Let's all stroke to - geth - er, __ like the Prince - ton

too. When you're good to Ma - ma, __
crew. When you're strok - in' Ma - ma, __

Ma - ma's good to you. __

Ma - ma's strok - in' you. __